AWARD-WINNI

Appliqué Birds

PAMELA HUMPHRIES

Located in Paducah, Kentucky, the American Quilter's Society (AQS) is dedicated to promoting the accomplishments of today's quilters. Through its publications and events, AQS strives to honor today's quiltmakers and their work and to inspire future creativity and innovation in quiltmaking.

Executive Editor: Nicole C. Chambers
Editor: Linda Baxter Lasco
Graphic Design: Lynda Smith
Cover Design: Michael Buckingham
Photography: Charles R. Lynch

Library of Congress Cataloging-in-Publication Data

Humphries, Pamela.
   Award-winning appliqué birds / by Pamela Humphries.
      p. cm.
   Summary: "Patterns to appliqué realistic and recognizable songbirds. Use all the patterns on a full-sized quilt or use individually. Lists for tools and supplies are provided. Patterns adapt to your favorite appliqué technique or follow author's instructions for peel-and-stick templates"--Provided by publisher.
   ISBN 978-1-57432-943-8
   1. Appliqué--Patterns. 2. Patchwork--Patterns. 3. Quilting--Patterns. I. Title.

   TT779.H865 2007
   746.44'5041--dc22

                                                2007032675

Additional copies of this book may be ordered from the American Quilter's Society, PO Box 3290, Paducah, KY 42002-3290, or online at www.AmericanQuilter.com. For phone orders only 800-626-5420. For all other inquiries, call 270-898-7903.

Proudly printed and bound in the United States of America.

Contents

In 1999, shortly after retiring from 32 years in the communications industry, I was introduced to the wonderful world of quilts. Through the magic of television, I discovered quilting as an expression of art in fabrics. I was fascinated with the fantastic displays of color and style and knew immediately that I had to make a quilt.

At a local quilt shop I attended a basic quilting class where everything was done by hand – piecing, appliqué and quilting – and I was hooked. I attended a few more classes on appliqué and hand quilting and started building my collection of quilting books. I read, practiced, tried various techniques, and made sample blocks for months trying to feel comfortable enough to actually begin a quilt.

Finally I was ready to start my first quilt. But what should it be? I was drawn to the Baltimore Album style but was intimidated by the complexity of the patterns. I decided to start small and drew on my longtime fascination with birds to select a theme. My first quilt was going to be a one-block wallhanging with a hummingbird and a few flowers. Appliquéing that first block was so much fun, I could not stop. After nine hummingbird blocks in a unique setting, a large ribbon-type border and lots of hand quilting, my first quilt, HUMMINGBIRD FANTASY, was completed. This wall quilt featured several of my original hummingbird designs and a combination of many commercial patterns.

For my next quilt, I wanted to continue with the birds and flowers theme but this time I wanted my birds to look as if they could fly off the quilt and visit my backyard feeders. So after studying lots of photographs, field guides, and other birding books, I drafted my designs. I then spent many wonderful months selecting fabrics and appliquéing these vibrant birds. I was so pleased with the results that I titled my quilt FEATHERED BEAUTIES, because these birds are true beauties. In April 2006, FEATHERED BEAUTIES won the AQS Hand Workmanship Award and now resides in the Museum of the American Quilter's Society in Paducah, Kentucky.

I hope you enjoy working with these birds as much as I have. These patterns can be used to make a variety of projects; from a small wallhanging with one or two blocks to a large bed quilt with lots of birds. Add your favorite flowers, vines, trees, or branches to create a design that is uniquely yours. Imagine the sparkle these beautiful birds will add to your next project.

Hand appliqué does not require a big investment in tools of the trade. If you are already a quilter or have done any sewing, you probably have most of what you need to get started. Listed below are my preferences in tools and thoughts on fabric selections.

Needles and Threader ◇ The most common needles used for hand appliqué are the milliner's or straw needle and the sharps needle. Both have slender shafts, but the milliner's needle is longer than the sharps. Many quilters like the extra length of the milliner's for turning under fabric as they appliqué. I find I can control the size of my stitches better with the sharps. My favorite appliqué needle is the Piecemakers® Hand Appliqué needle, which is a size 12 sharps.

One thing all appliqué needles have in common is a very small eye, so for me a needle threader is a real necessity. Most quilt shops carry needle threaders designed for small eye needles. I always keep several threaders on hand because without a threader, I can't stitch.

Pins ◇ Silk pins or appliqué pins with glass heads are ideal for hand appliqué. The silk pins are usually 1¼" or longer. Most appliqué pins are only ½" long although some brands are available in ¾" length.

Scissors ◇ There are lots of specialty scissors on the market today but you really need just three: a good sharp scissors for cutting fabric, one for cutting paper, and a small embroidery scissors for cutting threads and clipping inside seam allowances on curves.

Marking Tools ◇ Even if you are fairly new to quilting, you have probably already tried a variety of fabric marking tools. If you don't already have a favorite I suggest trying several types to see what works best for you. Please remember to always test the marker to ensure that it can be completely removed from the fabrics you are using.

I prefer a water-soluble marker with a fine tip. For light colored fabrics, I use a fine tipped blue marker. For dark colors, I like the Clover® white marking pen that can be removed with water or by ironing. Another marking tool I find very useful is the Clover Eraser Pen that removes blue, water-soluble marks. This is handy if you make a mistake when marking. You can erase and remark the design without having to wet the fabric then wait for it to dry before continuing.

Work Surface ◇ One of the nice things about hand appliqué is that it's so portable – you can pretty much take your project anywhere. Wherever you choose to appliqué, a portable work surface will be very helpful when positioning and pinning appliqué pieces or simply as a place to hold your scissors, needle threader, etc.

I use a sandpaper board, which is nothing more than a very fine grit sheet of sandpaper glued to a rigid board. The board can be anything such as heavy cardboard, a thin piece of wood, or even a plastic cutting board.

Light Box ◇ A light box is very useful for tracing patterns onto your fabric. Ready-made light boxes are available at many quilt and craft shops but you can easily make your own. All you need is a light source and a piece of glass or sturdy clear plastic.

Threads ◇ Use a good quality 100% cotton or silk thread in a color to match the appliqué fabric. Silk threads are a little more difficult to manage but the stitches are more easily hidden. I use both cotton and silk threads. For most appliqué fabrics I use Mettler®100% cotton #60 weight embroidery thread. It's a very fine thread and is available in a wide range of colors. For fabrics like batiks, where the appliqué stitches tend to show more, I use YLI® silk thread #100.

Tip

When washing and drying fabrics, do not use fabric softeners or dryer sheets. Instead of removing the "static cling," use the cling to help hold your fabrics in place as you stitch.

Fabrics ◇ Fabric selection is a very important aspect of any appliqué project. I recommend 100% cotton, high quality fabrics with an even, moderately tight weave. I also recommend prewashing all fabrics to remove any excess dye. Nothing will ruin a beautiful appliqué project as much as colors bleeding onto each other.

Background Fabrics ◇ Choose a background fabric that will provide good contrast to your appliqué motifs. Solids or nearly-solids in a light neutral color will make a good background for the projects in this book. Dark, bright, and even pastel appliqué fabrics will show up well against a light background.

In addition to contrast, consider how the background fabric will work with your quilting designs. Tone-on-tone background fabrics can add interest to your work, but these fabrics may not show off your quilting stitches as well as a solid fabric. My favorite background fabric is cotton sateen in off-white or light cream. Cotton sateen is very soft, has a beautiful sheen, and is ideal for hand quilting.

Appliqué Fabrics ◇ Let the look you are trying to create guide you in fabric selection. For the bird patterns in this book, textured and tonal fabrics can bring your birds to life. If you are going for the realistic look, nature has already selected the color scheme so all you have to do is focus on the texture and feel of the fabric.

When selecting fabrics try to look past the overall design and look closely at small patches of the fabric visualizing how these patches could work for the various parts of the bird. Marbled, splotchy, and speckled fabrics frequently work well for the head, body, and under parts of a bird. Fabrics with a linear or streaked texture are good candidates for the wing and tail sections. Large-scale prints and florals can offer interesting possibilities.

About the Patterns

Twenty-four bird patterns are presented as complete, individual birds allowing you the most flexibility in creating your own unique design. Several of the sample blocks have one bird overlapping another. In these instances, a dashed outline on the pattern indicates placement of the partly covered bird. There are also five full block patterns designed for 12-inch blocks set on point.

All of the patterns depict the size of each bird as it appears on the quilt. You can easily enlarge or reduce these patterns to any size you choose. You will need to enlarge them if you want the birds to be life-sized.

These patterns are suitable for any appliqué technique. The pattern pieces are numbered as in traditional appliqué; however, the associated instructions are for using the pre-appliqué method described later.

Block & Project Designs

Many quilters like to plan their entire project in advance; others like myself prefer to begin with a basic concept and a single block then build from there using a plan-as-you-go technique. Whatever method you choose there are several things to consider before you begin.

Block size and setting is one of the first decisions to make, as this is difficult if not impossible to change as you go. Since these appliqué birds are definitely directional, a block designed for a straight set will probably not work if you later change to an on-point setting. It's also a good idea to cut your background fabric two or three inches larger than the block design to allow flexibility in designing your sashings.

Another consideration to address in the planning stage is quilting space. If you want to incorporate quilted motifs into your project, remember to allow sufficient space for this in your original plan. When I made my first hand appliquéd quilt, HUMMINGBIRD FANTASY, I was so into hand appliqué that I filled the entire quilt top with appliqué. It wasn't until the top was finished and I was ready to quilt that I realized there was no space for pretty quilting designs. Since I enjoy hand quilting as much as hand appliqué, I was very disappointed. Looking back, I'm not sure I would have changed my original design to allow room for quilting, but now I do consider quilting designs in the planning process.

Designing your own projects can be a fun and rewarding experience. You don't have to be an artist or experienced in drafting to create your own original designs. Try these simple steps using cutouts to design an appliqué block around one or more birds from this book.

1. Begin with a sheet of paper larger than what you need to fit the entire block. Add lines to indicate the edges.

2. Choose the bird/birds you wish to use. Copy the patterns onto tracing paper and cut out each bird leaving a half-inch space around the pattern.

3. Choose some of your favorite flower patterns to include in the design, copy the patterns onto tracing paper, and cut out each flower.

4. Arrange bird and flower cutouts on your paper block until you find a design that pleases you. Secure cutouts in place with small pieces of tape.

5. Place a large piece of tracing paper over the entire block and tape it in place. Sketch in a few branches and vines. Various sizes and thicknesses will enhance your design. Don't worry if your lines are not completely smooth because in nature branches are full of lumps and bumps.

6. Add some leaves. You can sketch these onto the same layer as the branches and vines or, if you prefer, make cutouts like you did for the birds and flowers.

7. When you are satisfied with your design, place another sheet of tracing paper over all layers and trace all elements onto the single sheet to complete the block design.

8. To preview your design in color, place another sheet of tracing paper over the completed design and fill in with colored pencils. By using extra sheets of tracing paper you can try various colors without affecting your original block drawing.

Appliqué Techniques

There are many methods and techniques for appliqué today; however, hand-appliqué techniques can be grouped into two broad categories:

Prepared Seam Appliqué ◇ Prepared seam appliqué refers to any method where the seams are folded under then basted, glued, or ironed in place before the piece is appliquéd to the background fabric. Freezer paper positioned on the wrong side of the appliqué fabric is commonly used as the template for these methods. The template remains in place until the piece is appliquéd then removed by slitting the background fabric.

Needle-Turn Appliqué ◇ With needle turn appliqué, the seams are turned under with the needle as you sew. Using this method, the pattern can be drawn on the right side of the fabric or a paper template (freezer paper or stick-on paper) can be positioned on the right side of the fabric. The piece is then appliquéd along the drawn line or the edge of the paper template.

This is a very simplified description of hand appliqué techniques and does not address all of the possibilities. If you are new to appliqué, I encourage you to take a class, read books, and experiment with various techniques until you find what suits you best.

I most frequently use needle-turn appliqué using "peel-and-stick" labels as templates. For complex motifs like the birds, I also like to pre-construct or pre-appliqué the individual pieces together into a unit and then appliqué the completed units to the background fabric.

Things to know about peel-and-stick templates ◇

I prefer to use the peel-and-stick labels rather than freezer paper especially when working with several small appliqué pieces. The labels are easier to remove and reposition and do not require ironing. I use white 8½" x 11" full sheet labels designed for use in ink-jet printers. These are generally available at any store that carries office supplies.

Transfer the pattern to the front of the label. This can be accomplished by

◇ using a light box to trace the pattern, including piece numbers, to the label;

◇ using a copy machine to copy the pattern to the label; or

◇ scanning the pattern into your computer and then printing on the label.

Carefully cut out the individual pattern pieces. Peel off the backing and stick the template to the right side of the appliqué fabric. Take time to position the template on the exact piece of fabric you want to use. For example, if you want a blue feather with a darker blue tip, use a fabric with varying shades of blue and place the template so that the tip of the feather is on a darker blue than the rest of the feather. With judicious template placement, you can achieve incredible results making your appliqué appear much more complex than it actually is.

Cut out the appliqué piece leaving a ¼" seam allowance around the piece. This allows for easier handling of small pieces and will later be trimmed to ⅛" as it is appliquéd.

Pre-Appliqué ◇

Pre-appliqué is very useful for appliqué designs with many small pieces. Instead of having to position and appliqué several small pieces to the background, you can appliqué them together and then position and stitch this larger combined piece to the background fabric. Pre-appliqué also gives a smoother appearance to the finished design.

In regular appliqué, each piece is applied to the background in sequence beginning with the piece that will appear farthest from you and ending with the piece that appears closest to you. Patterns are generally numbered in this manner.

In pre-appliqué, this same numbering sequence is used but you have the flexibility of working in either ascending or descending order. When using descending sequence, begin with the highest numbered piece for the section and pre-appliqué to the next lower numbered piece. Continue until all pieces in the section are completed.

Pre-appliqué in descending sequence using peel-and-stick templates is a very forgiving method of appliqué.

In the following example, fabric was prepared with peel-and-stick templates as described previously. The sample unit is for the tail section of the bird (figure 1).

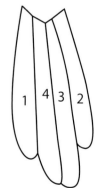

Figure 1. Tail pattern

 Beginnning with piece 4, position piece 4 over piece 3 and pin into place. On the edge that joins piece 3, fold under and lightly finger press the long stitching line.

Mark the starting and ending points on template 4. You can do this by creasing it with your fingernail or marking with a pencil (figure 2, page 10). It is important to start and end your stitching at the seam lines. Do not stitch into the seam allowance.

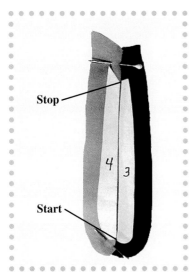

Figure 2. Pieces pinned and marked with start/ stop points

3. Temporarily remove template 3 and set aside. It will make it easier to appliqué. You will reuse template 3 later so keep it in a safe place.

4. Appliqué piece 4 to piece 3 making sure the start and stop points are firmly secured.

5. Stick template 3 back into place. If your fabric shifted slightly during appliqué, template 3 can be repositioned to achieve the correct placement.

6. Turn the piece over and trim the seam allowance to slightly less than ⅛".

7. Appliqué the combined piece 4–3 to piece 2, following steps 1 through 6 above. Repeat to appliqué piece 4–3–2 to piece 1.

8. The tail section is now completed and ready to be appli-quéd as a single unit to the background fabric (figure 3).

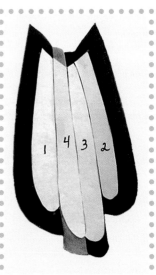

Figure 3. Complete, pre-appliquéd tail section

This is the appliqué method I recommend for all the patterns in this book. For the bird patterns, I pre-appliqué in sections then appliqué each section to the background fabric. Generally, birds are organized into tail, upper wing, lower wing, head, and body sections. Along with each pattern, you will find details on the pre-appliqué sections and sequences.

Yardage — Quilt Size 70" x 84"

Background ◇ 5⅞ yards

Scraps ◇ see individual patterns

Sashing insets ◇ 1 yard

Sashing bias ◇ 1½ yards

Inner border ◇ 1 yard

Outer border ◇ 2¾ yards

Backing ◇ 5½ yards

Batting ◇ 78" x 92"

Binding ◇ ⅝ yard

From the background fabric, cut nine 14" squares for the center blocks.

Fold the squares in quarters and lightly press with an iron. These folds will be your guidelines for centering the appliqué.

Appliqué the nine central blocks and square up the blocks to measure 12½".

Arrange the blocks in three rows of three blocks each, as shown in figure 1. Make sure the orientation of your blocks matches the illustration.

Sew the blocks into rows; press. Sew the rows together. Press again.

Using the template and instructions on page 89, cut 24 sashing insets. Baste the sashing insets in place, centering them over the seams joining the blocks (figure 2). Leave the parts that extend beyond the outer edge of the nine-block unit free.

Each sashing inset requires approximately 36" of ⅜" (finished) bias tape to secure it in place.

Referring to figure 3 on page 12, appliqué the bias tape, as illustrated. Remember to leave the areas that extend beyond the edge of the nine-block unit free.

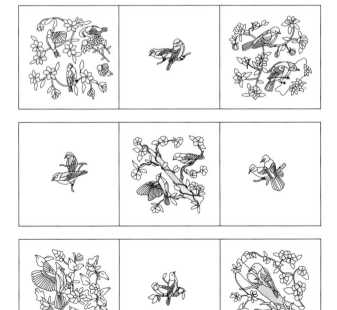

Figure 1.

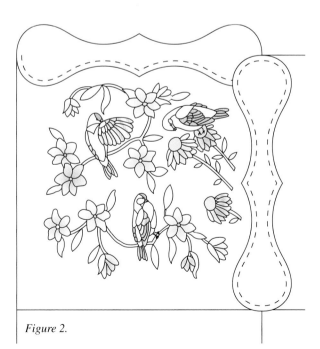

Figure 2.

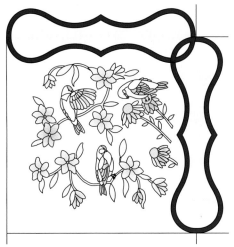

Figure 3.

Background

Cut two background panels 40" x 65". Join with a seam to form a panel 79½" x 65". Press the seam allowance open.

Center the nine-block unit on the background, aligning the points of the leftmost and far right blocks with the center seam (figure 4). Pin or baste in place.

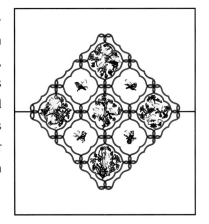

Figure 4.

Secure the nine-block unit by basting the free edges of the outer sashing insets to the background. Appliqué the sashing bias tape in place. Then, appliqué the four corner birds and the floral and vine border to the quilt (pages 78–87).

Borders

Appliqué the inner and outer borders to the four sides of the quilt, then join all of the borders at the corners using a mitered seam. Enough yardage is given to cut the outer border strips lengthwise.

To make the inner border, measure the length and width of the quilt through the center and add 9" to these measurements. Cut a piece of freezer paper for both lengths. Label the freezer paper and fold it in half lengthwise, shiny sides together. Cut two fabric strips for each piece of freezer paper.

Refer to page 91 and trace the inner and outer border scallop curves onto the freezer-paper templates for both the sides and top/bottom of the quilt. Arrange the curves for each template as indicated in the illustration. Cut out along the drawn lines keeping freezer paper folded in half.

Unfold the freezer paper and match the center point of the templates to the center point of the corresponding inner border fabric strip. Place the paper template ½" from the edge of the fabric. Mark scallops on the right side of the fabric.

Center the marked inner border along the side of the quilt, overlapping the border enough so that there is at least ½" seam allowance under the deepest curves. Baste the inner border strip in place. Trim the scallops, leaving only a scant ¼" seam allowance as you appliqué the inner border to the side of the quilt. When finished, trim away the excess background fabric from beneath the scallops. Repeat for the other side and the top and bottom of the quilt.

To make the outer border, measure the length and width of the quilt and add 17" to these measurements. Repeat the steps you used for the inner border to mark and appliqué the outer border to the quilt. Be sure you are using the scallop curves for the outer border

Join the borders at the corners with a mitered seam. Trim the corner seam allowance to measure ¼".

Trim the background from behind the nine-block center unit to reduce bulk. Layer backing, batting, and quilt top. Quilt as desired. Bind, label, and enjoy your quilt!

Feathered Beauties, 70" x 84" made by the author

American Goldfinch

The American Goldfinch, sometimes referred to as a wild canary, is a small, colorful bird plentiful in most areas of the United States. It favors hulled sunflower and thistle seeds and will readily visit feeders where these are provided. The American Goldfinch is the state bird of Iowa, New Jersey, and Washington.

Male American Goldfinch 1

Fabrics

Pieces: 1–5 • 9–11 • 24–26 ◆ Black-and-white textured. Position fabrics so each feather is mostly black with some white along the outside edge.

Pieces: 17–23 • 27–29 • 34 ◆ Shades of black lightly textured with white or gray. Position fabrics so that white or gray highlights are scattered throughout the feathers.

Piece: 6 ◆ Light gray

Piece: 7 ◆ Very pale yellow

Pieces: 8 • 12 • 14–15 • 30–33 • 35 ◆ Shades of yellow

Piece: 13 ◆ Golden brown

Piece: 16 ◆ Black

Embroidery:
Satin stitch in black for the eye. Stem stitch in light brown across the beak.

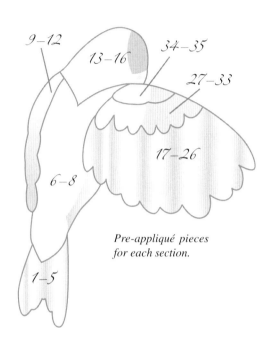

Pre-appliqué pieces for each section.

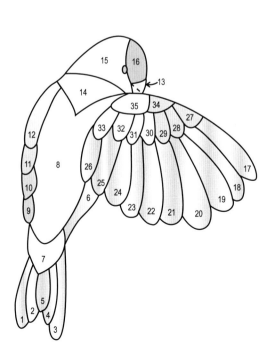

Male American Goldfinch 2

Fabrics

Pieces: 1–4 • 24–25 ◆ Black-and-white textured. Position fabrics so each feather is mostly black with some white along the outside edge.

Pieces: 7–9 • 19–23 ◆ Shades of black lightly textured with white or gray

Piece: 5–6 • 10 • 12–15 • 18 • 26
◆ Shades of light and medium yellow

Piece: 11 ◆ Yellowish brown

Pieces: 16 ◆ Black

Piece: 17 ◆ Light brown

Embroidery:
Satin stitch in black for the eye. Stem stitch in medium brown across beak. Use a double row of stem stitches in medium brown for the legs and feet.

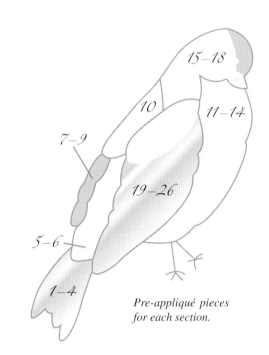

Pre-appliqué pieces
for each section.

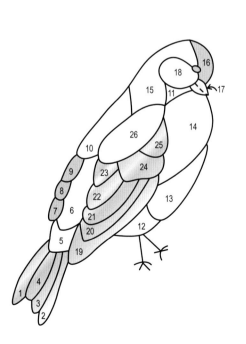

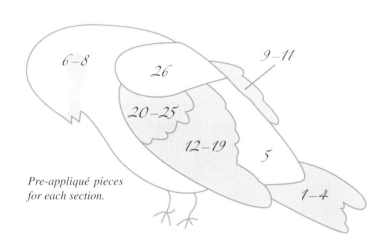

Pre-appliqué pieces for each section.

Female American Goldfinch

Fabrics

Pieces: 1–4 • 9–11 ◆ Black-and-white textured. Position fabrics so each feather is mostly black with some white along the outside edge.

Piece: 19–25 ◆ Black with white splotches. Position fabrics so that the lower edge of each feather is white.

Pieces: 12–18 ◆ Shades of black lightly textured with white or gray

Piece: 5–6 ◆ Light yellow

Pieces: 7 • 26 ◆ Light brown, preferably with yellowish tint.

Piece: 8 ◆ Medium brown

Embroidery:
Satin stitch in black for the eye. Satin stitch in light brown for the beak. Use a double row of stem stitches in medium brown for the legs and feet.

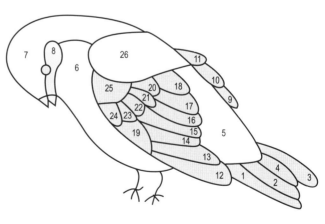

Fabrics:

Select a variety of colors and textures for the flowers. For some of the star-shaped flowers a thin, soft-edged stripe down the center of each petal can add an interesting effect.

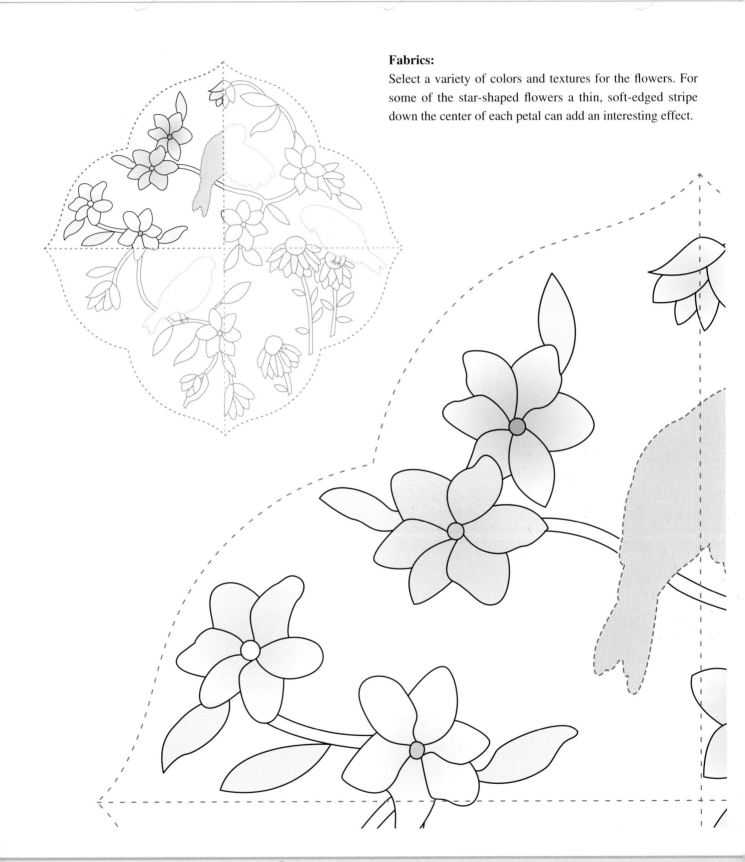

Appliqué Notes:

The stems are designed for ⅛" finished bias strips but ¼" strips will also work. A few of the leaves may have to be repositioned to accommodate the larger stems.

Individual flowers can be pre-appliquéd then applied to the background as a completed unit. Small flower centers can be embroidered with a satin stitch.

The Northern Cardinal is a popular and easily recognized backyard visitor. Seven states have adopted this red beauty as their state bird – Kentucky, Illinois, Indiana, North Carolina, Ohio, Virginia, and West Virginia.

Male Northern Cardinal

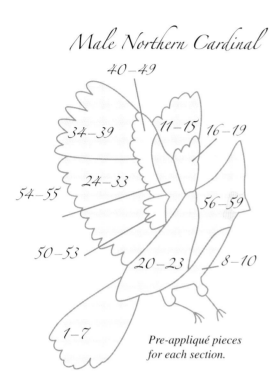

Pre-appliqué pieces for each section.

Fabrics:

Pieces: 1–3 • 5 • 24–39 ◆ Red with streaks of black or dark brown. Position fabrics so that the dark streaks run along the length of the feathers.

Pieces: 40 • 55 ◆ Red with streaks of black or dark brown. Position fabrics so that the dark streaks parallel the top edge of the wing.

Pieces: 20 • 54 ◆ Brown

Pieces: 42–43 • 47–50 ◆ Medium reddish orange

Pieces: 41 • 44–46 • 51–53 ◆ Light reddish orange

Pieces: 7–9 • 19 • 21 ◆ Dark red

Pieces: 6 • 10 • 11–14 • 18 • 57 • 59 ◆ Medium red

Pieces: 4 • 15–17 ◆ Light red

Pieces: 22–23 ◆ Reddish brown

Piece: 56 ◆ Medium brown

Piece: 58 ◆ Black

Embroidery:

Satin stitch in black for the eye. Satin stitch across the beak in a dark brown. Use a triple row of stem stitches in medium brown for the legs and feet.

Female Northern Cardinal

Fabrics:

Pieces: 1–6 ◆ Red with streaks of black or dark brown. Position fabrics so that the dark streaks run along the length of the feathers.

Pieces: 7 • 9 ◆ White or very light tan

Piece: 8 ◆ Light rust

Pieces: 10 • 15 ◆ Red

Piece: 12 ◆ Light red or peach

Piece: 11 ◆ Light brown

Piece: 13 ◆ Black

Piece: 14 ◆ Medium rust

Embroidery:

Satin stitch in black for the eye. Satin stitch across the beak in a medium brown. Use a double or triple row of stem stitches in medium brown for the legs and feet.

Pre-appliqué pieces for each section.

Male Northern Cardinal

Female Northern Cardinal

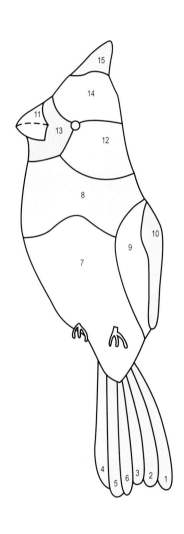

Fabrics:

Select a variety of colors and textures for the flowers.

Appliqué Notes:

Notice that a branch is in front of the female cardinal, so appliqué the bird first then add the branch.

The leaves in this block are fairly large and will look better if they are divided into two sections. You can create this division by using different fabrics for each side of the leaf. You can also use a single fabric and embroider a vein down the center of the leaf.

Eastern Bluebirds are frequent backyard visitors across the eastern part of the United States. They are often seen in mating pairs. Birders throughout the country are helping increase the population of these beautiful birds by providing nesting boxes in suburban areas.

Male Eastern Bluebird

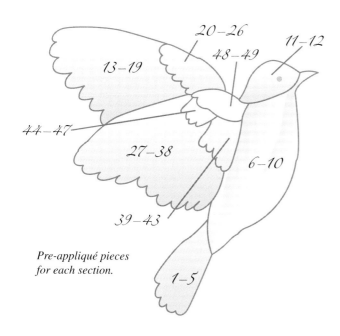

Pre-appliqué pieces for each section.

Fabrics:

Pieces: 1 • 3–4 • 10 • 12 • 13 • 17–20 • 23–25 ◆ Shades of dark blue

Pieces: 5 • 11 • 14–16 • 21–22 • 26 • 31–34 • 36–38 • 42 • 44–45 ◆ Shades of medium blue

Pieces: 2 • 27–30 • 35 • 39–41 • 43 • 46–49 ◆ Shades of light blue

Piece: 7 ◆ Light gray

Piece: 6 ◆ Medium gray

Pieces: 8–9 ◆ Rust

Embroidery:
Satin stitch in black for the eye. Satin stitch the beak in a medium brown.

Female Eastern Bluebird

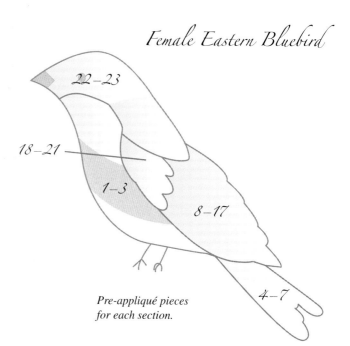

Pre-appliqué pieces for each section.

Fabrics

Pieces: 6 • 8 • 12 • 15 ◆ Shades of dark blue

Pieces: 4 • 7 • 10 • 13 • 17 ◆ Shades of medium blue

Pieces: 5 • 11 • 14 • 16 ◆ Shades of light blue

Pieces: 9 • 18–21 ◆ Blue gray

Piece: 1 ◆ Very light gray – almost white

Pieces: 22–23 ◆ Gray

Piece: 2 ◆ Light rust

Piece: 3 ◆ Medium rust

Embroidery:
Satin stitch in black for the eye. Satin stitch the beak in a medium brown. Use a double row of stem stitches in brown for the legs and feet.

Male Eastern Bluebird

Female Eastern Bluebird

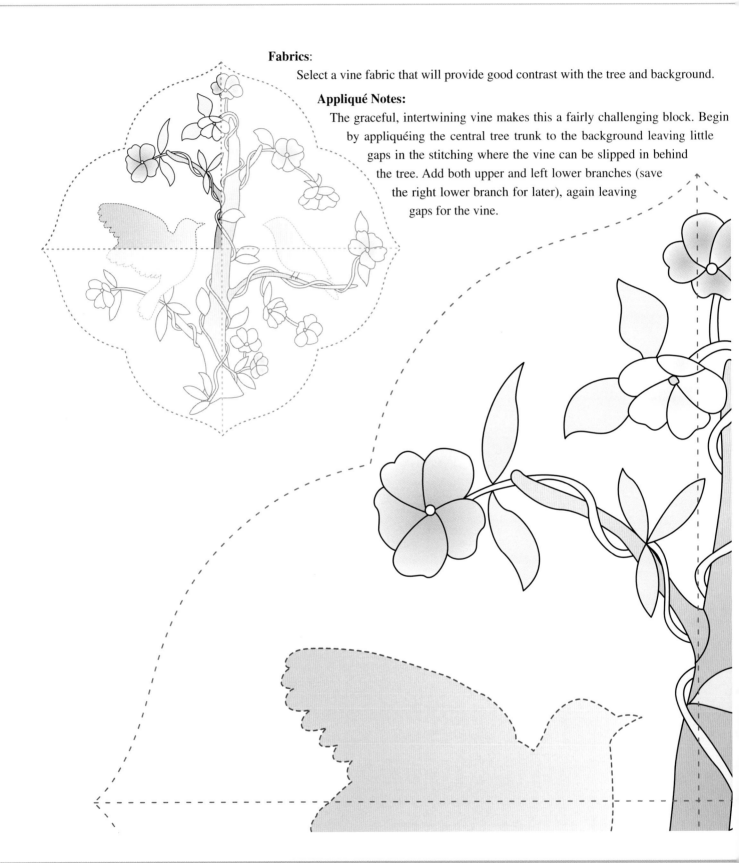

Fabrics:

Select a vine fabric that will provide good contrast with the tree and background.

Appliqué Notes:

The graceful, intertwining vine makes this a fairly challenging block. Begin by appliquéing the central tree trunk to the background leaving little gaps in the stitching where the vine can be slipped in behind the tree. Add both upper and left lower branches (save the right lower branch for later), again leaving gaps for the vine.

Using ⅛" bias strips prepared with bias bars, appliqué the vine following the pattern design and tucking ends behind the tree trunk and branches. Fill in any remaining stitching gaps on the tree.

Since the remaining branch is in front of the female bluebird, first appliqué the bird, then add the branch and vine. Add the leaves, flowers, and the male bluebird and your block is complete.

Baltimore Oriole

Baltimore Orioles, strikingly beautiful in their bright orange and black plumage, are summertime visitors to most of the eastern US and Canada. They forage mainly for insects and nectar and will occasionally try to sip from hummingbird feeders. Many backyard bird watchers now use oriole feeders, which are a larger version of the hummingbird feeder, to accommodate the oriole's larger size.

Male Baltimore Oriole

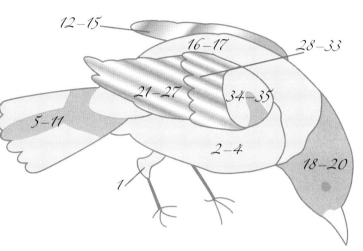

Pre-appliqué pieces for each section.

Fabrics:

Piece: 10 ◆ Black with white or gray highlights

Pieces: 15 • 19–20 • 35 ◆ Black

Piece: 18 ◆ Gray

Pieces: 1–4 • 11 • 16–17 • 34 ◆ Shades of orange preferably with yellow highlights

Pieces: 12–14 • 28–32 ◆ Black with white. Position so that some white is along the bottom tip of each feather.

Pieces: 21–27 • 33 ◆ Black with white. Position so that white is along the right and bottom edges of each feather.

Pieces: 5–9 ◆ Orange with black at base of tail. Since orange and black fabrics can be difficult to find, you can stitch a black fabric to an orange fabric and press the seam open. Then using permanent black ink or black embroidery thread, make a few short lines across the seam line to soften the effect. Position templates with the dotted line across the seam line.

Embroidery:

Satin stitch in black for the eye and outline with light gray stem stitches. Stem stitch in dark gray across the beak. Use a triple row of stem stitches in gray for the legs and feet.

Fabrics:

Pieces: 5 • 16 ◆ Brown

Piece: 15 ◆ Gray

Pieces: 12 • 14 ◆ Yellow orange

Pieces: 1 • 6 • 10 • 13 ◆ Light orange

Pieces: 2–4 • 17 • 31 ◆ Medium orange

Piece: 11 ◆ Dark orange

Pieces: 7–9 • 23–30 ◆ Black with white. Position so that some white is along the bottom tip of each feather.

Pieces: 18–22 ◆ Black with white. Position so that white is along the outside and bottom edges of each feather.

Embroidery:

Satin stitch in black for the eye. Stem stitch in dark gray across the beak. Use a triple row of stem stitches in gray for the leg and foot.

Female Baltimore Oriole

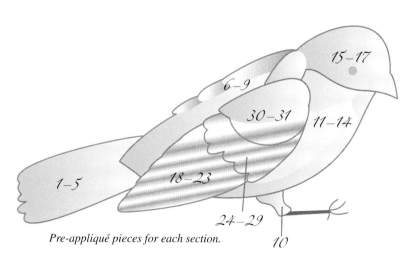

Pre-appliqué pieces for each section.

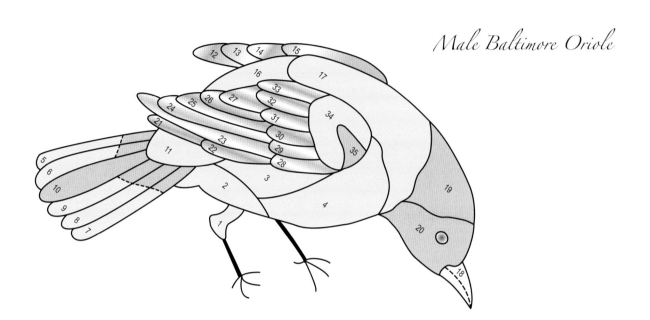

Male Baltimore Oriole

Female Baltimore Oriole

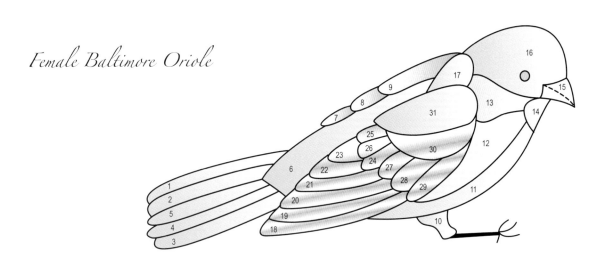

Fabrics:

Select a textured fabric that resembles grass or bare ground for the patch under the male oriole. Combine light, medium, and dark-toned petals to create interesting flowers.

Appliqué Notes:

Begin by appliquéing the branches, stems, and leaves to the background fabric. Use ¼" bias strips for the main branches and ⅛" bias strips for the smaller ones.

Petals of each flower can be pre-appliquéd and applied to the background as a completed unit. Then, appliqué the sepals or the green parts at the base of the flower to the background.

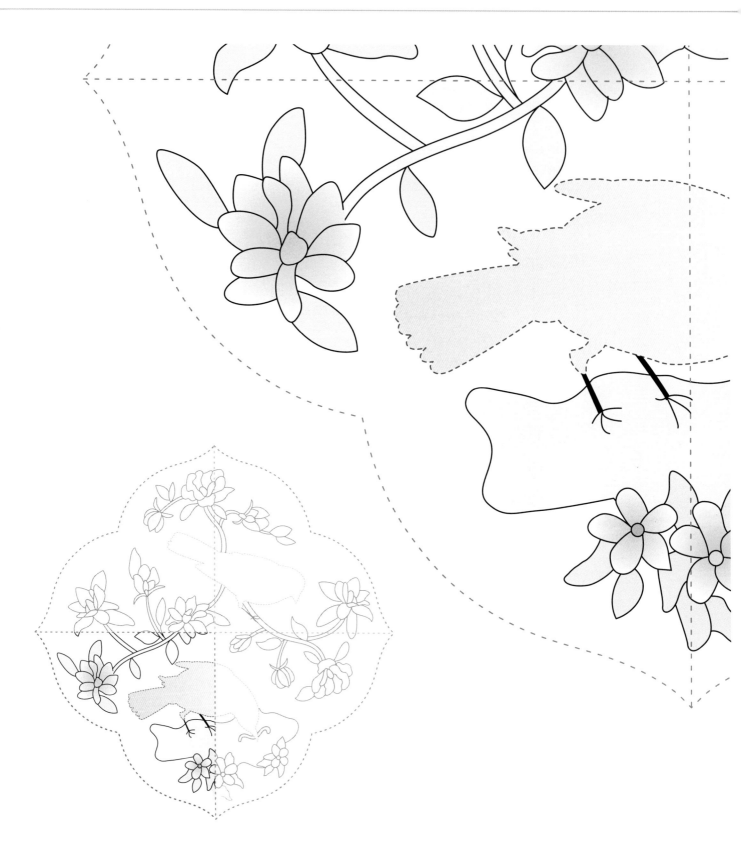

The Red-headed Woodpecker can be found throughout the eastern United States. Although populations are declining they are still abundant in the open forests of the midwest. Their diet consists mainly of nuts, fruit, corn, and insects, and occasional visits to backyard bird and squirrel feeders.

Red-headed Woodpecker ◆ *Red-headed Woodpecker* ◆ *Red-headed Woodpecker*
-headed Woodpecker ◆ *Red-headed Woodpecker* ◆ *Red-headed Woodpecker* ◆ *R*
pecker ◆ *Red-headed Woodpecker* ◆ *Red-headed Woodpecker* ◆ *Red-headed W.*

Red-headed Woodpecker

Fabrics

Pieces: 2–3 ◆ Brown
Pieces: 1 • 6 • 11–12 • 15 • 20 • 22 • 25 ◆ Black
Pieces: 7–9 • 19 • 21 • 23–24 • 26–28 ◆ Black
with small white or light gray highlights
Pieces: 13–14 • 16–18 ◆ White
Pieces: 4–5 • 10 ◆ White with black or dark gray
highlights
Piece: 29 ◆ Dark gray
Piece: 30 ◆ Red

Embroidery:
Satin stitch in black for the eye.

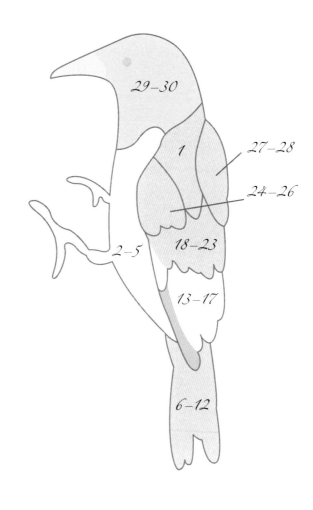

Pre-appliqué pieces for each section.

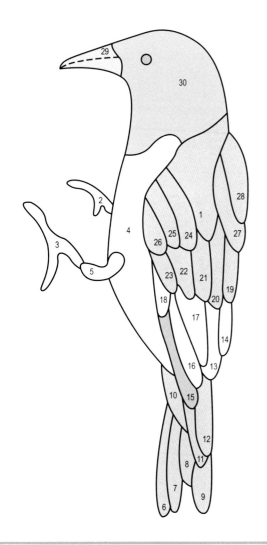

Red-headed Woodpecker ◇ Red-headed Woodpecker ◇ Red-headed Woodpe
Red-headed Woodpecker ◇ Red-headed Woodpecker ◇ Red-headed Woodpecker ◇
oodpecker ◇ Red-headed Woodpecker ◇ Red-headed Woodpecker ◇ Red-headed

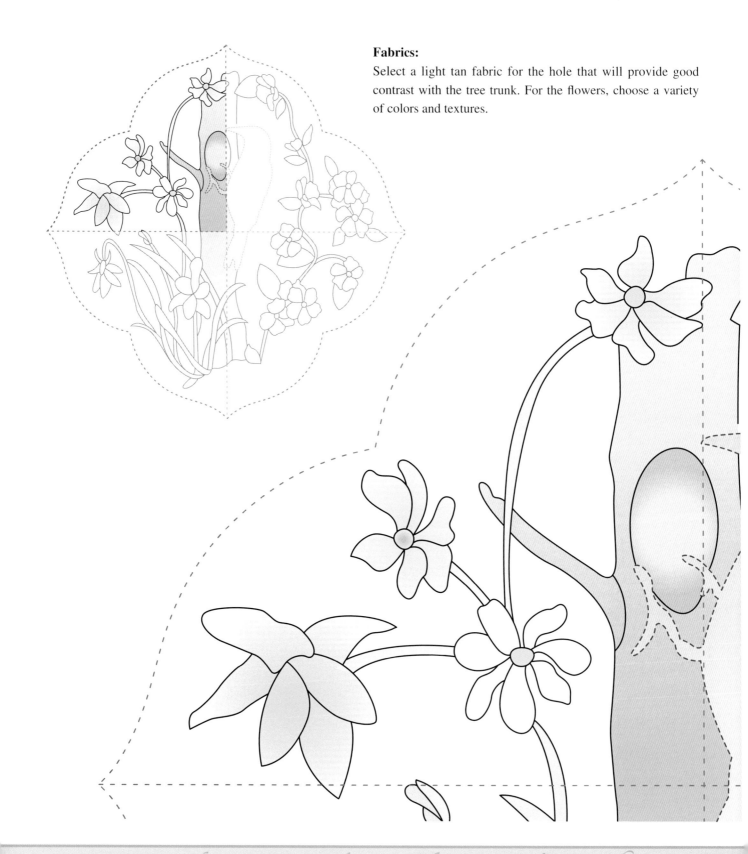

Fabrics:

Select a light tan fabric for the hole that will provide good contrast with the tree trunk. For the flowers, choose a variety of colors and textures.

Red-headed Woodpecker ◆ Red-headed Woodpecker ◆ Red-headed Woodpecker
-headed Woodpecker ◆ Red-headed Woodpecker ◆ Red-headed Woodpecker ◆ R
pecker ◆ Red-headed Woodpecker ◆ Red-headed Woodpecker ◆ Red-headed W

Appliqué Notes:

Use reverse appliqué for the hole in the tree trunk to create depth. Cut out the hole in the tree fabric leaving a ⅛" to ¼" seam allowance on the inside of the hole.

Fold under the seam allowance along the stitching line, clipping as necessary so that it lies flat.

Pin the hole fabric behind the tree fabric and appliqué in place.

Red-headed Woodpecker ◆ Red-headed Woodpecker ◆ Red-headed Woodpecker ◆ Red-headed Woodp
Red-headed Woodpecker ◆ Red-headed Woodpecker ◆ Red-headed Woodpecker ◆
oodpecker ◆ Red-headed Woodpecker ◆ Red-headed Woodpecker ◆ Red-headed

◈ *Red-headed Woodpecker* ◈ *Red-headed Woodpecker* ◈ *Red-headed Woodpecker*
-headed Woodpecker ◈ *Red-headed Woodpecker* ◈ *Red-headed Woodpecker* ◈ *R*
pecker ◈ *Red-headed Woodpecker* ◈ *Red-headed Woodpecker* ◈ *Red-headed We*

Western & Summer Tanagers

The Western Tanager is distinctive with its bright red head, yellow body, and black back and wings. Fairly common throughout the western United States, the Western Tanager is one of over 200 species of tanagers. Its close cousin, the Summer Tanager, is sometimes called the Bee Bird because of its fondness for eating bees and wasps.

Western Tanager

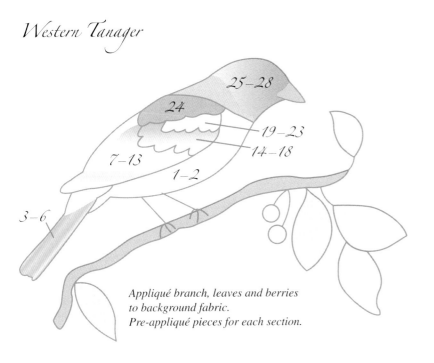

Appliqué branch, leaves and berries
to background fabric.
Pre-appliqué pieces for each section.

Fabrics

Pieces: 1–2 • 6–7 • 19–23 ◆ Shades of light and medium yellow

Pieces: 3–5 • 8–12 ◆ Black and white. Position fabric so that white is on the outside edge of each feather.

Pieces: 13–18 ◆ Black and white. Position fabric so that white is on the tip of each feather.

Piece: 24 ◆ Black

Piece: 25 ◆ Very dark gray

Piece: 26 ◆ Light red with pale splotches

Piece: 27 ◆ Light gray

Piece: 28 ◆ Medium red

Embroidery:
Satin stitch in black for the eye. Stem stitch in medium gray across the beak. Use a double row of stem stitches in dark gray for the legs and feet.

Summer Tanager

Fabrics

Pieces: 1 • 24 ◆ Light red

Pieces: 3–4 • 26 ◆ Medium red

Pieces: 5 • 9–10 • 13 ◆ Bright dark red

Pieces: 2 • 11–12 • 14–15 • 22 ◆ Dark red with tan or brown highlights

Pieces: 6–8 • 16–21 • 25 ◆ Reddish brown

Piece: 23 ◆ Tan

Embroidery:
Satin stitch in black for the eye. Stem stitch in light brown across the beak. Use a double row of stem stitches in medium brown for the feet.

Appliqué branch, leaves, berries, and bird
piece 1 directly to background fabric.
Pre-appliqué pieces for each section.

Western Tanager

Summer Tanager

Blue Jay

The Blue Jay is abundant throughout the eastern United States and Canada and will readily visit backyard feeders. Blue Jays are generally noisy and have the ability to make a variety of sounds, often mimicking other birds. The male and female are identical in appearance.

Blue Jay

Fabrics

Pieces: 1–3 ◆ Very light blue preferably with some white splotches

Pieces: 7 • 31–36 ◆ White

Pieces: 5–6 • 9 ◆ Black

Pieces: 4 • 8 • 19 • 38–39 ◆ Shades of medium blue

Pieces: 17–18 • 37 ◆ Shades of dark blue

Pieces: 10–11 • 13–14 • 16 • 25 • 27–28 • 30 ◆ Shades of medium blue with white. Position so white is on tip of feathers.

Pieces: 12 • 15 • 20–24 • 26 • 29 ◆ Shades of dark blue with white. Position so white is on tip of feathers.

Embroidery:
Satin stitch in black for the eye. Stem stitch in gray across the beak. Use triple row of stem stitches in dark gray for the leg and foot.

Finding blue and white fabrics in the desired shades can be difficult. As an alternative, you can use white fabric paint for the feather tips. Begin with the blue fabrics you selected. Using short brush strokes, make several small white patches on the fabric. Follow the paint manufacturer's instructions for setting the paint. The black wing bars can be added using permanent black ink.

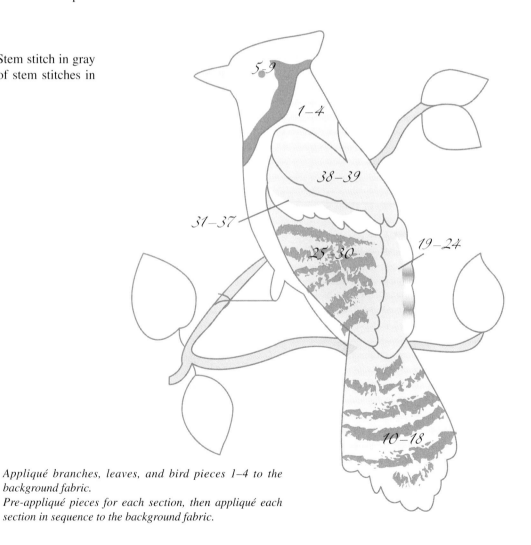

Appliqué branches, leaves, and bird pieces 1–4 to the background fabric.
Pre-appliqué pieces for each section, then appliqué each section in sequence to the background fabric.

Blue Jay

The Mountain Bluebird is frequently found in high mountain meadows and urban areas. Their brilliant sky blue coloring makes them easy to identify. Like other bluebirds, the Mountain Bluebird population is increasing because of the trails of nesting boxes set up by birders throughout the western part of the country.

Male Mountain Bluebird

Fabrics:

All of the fabrics for this bird are bright blue in shades ranging from very light to dark. Textured fabrics with white, gray, and dark highlights work best.

Pieces: 3 • 7 ◆ Very light
Pieces: 2 • 4 • 6 • 12 • 16 • 20 ◆ Light
Pieces: 1 • 5 • 10–11 • 15 • 17–18 • 21 ◆ Medium
Pieces: 8–9 • 13–14 • 19 ◆ Dark

Embroidery:

Satin stitch in black for the eye. Satin stitch the beak in a medium brown. Use a double row of stem stitches in medium brown for the leg and foot.

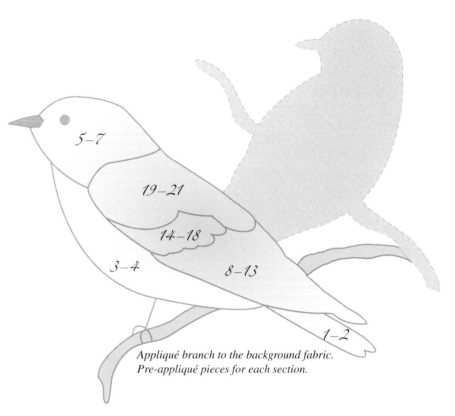

Appliqué branch to the background fabric.
Pre-appliqué pieces for each section.

Female Mountain Bluebird

Fabrics:

Pieces: 1–2 ◆ Very light gray
Pieces: 4 • 26 ◆ Light gray
Pieces: 3 • 25 ◆ Medium gray
Piece: 9 ◆ Light blue
Pieces: 5 • 7 • 16–18 • 22 ◆ Shades of light blue textured with dark blue highlights
6 • 8 • 10–15 • 19–21 • 23–24 ◆ Shades of medium blue textured with dark highlights. Position fabrics so that the lower or outside edge of each feather has some dark blue.

Embroidery:

Satin stitch in black for the eye. Satin stitch the beak in a medium brown.

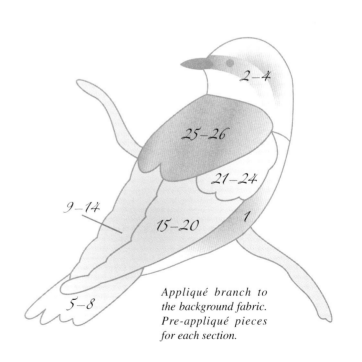

Appliqué branch to
the background fabric.
Pre-appliqué pieces
for each section.

Male Mountain Bluebird

Female Mountain Bluebird

The Vermilion Flycatcher can be found in the southwestern United States and throughout most of Mexico. It favors woody or brushy areas near ponds and streams. The male is very distinctive with bright red and black plumage. The female is mostly brown with just a touch of pink on the underbelly.

Male Vermilion Flycatcher

Fabrics
Pieces: 7–8 • 24 • 27 ◆ Shades of bright red
Piece: 9 ◆ Dark red
Pieces: 1–3 • 16–18 • 20–22 ◆ Black with small white or gray highlights
Pieces: 10–15 • 19 • 23 • 25–26 ◆ Shades of black
Pieces: 4–6 ◆ White

Embroidery:
Satin stitch in black for the eye. Outline the eye with light gray stem stitches. Use a double row of stem stitches in dark gray for the legs and feet.

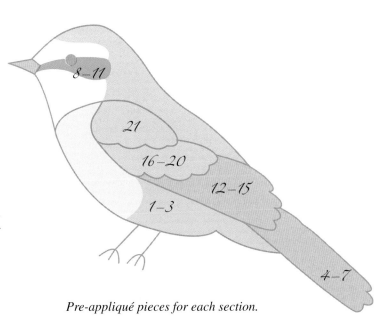

Appliqué branch to background.
Pre-appliqué pieces for each section.

Female Vermilion Flycatcher

Fabrics
Pieces: 1–2 ◆ Pink
Piece: 3 ◆ Light Tan
Pieces: 8–9 ◆ White
Pieces: 10 • 16–21 ◆ Light brown textures
Piece: 11 ◆ Medium brown
Piece: 15 ◆ Gray
Pieces: 4–7 • 12–14 ◆ Black with white or gray highlights

Embroidery:
Satin stitch in black for the eye and dark brown for the beak. Use a double row of stem stitches in dark brown for the legs and feet.

Pre-appliqué pieces for each section.

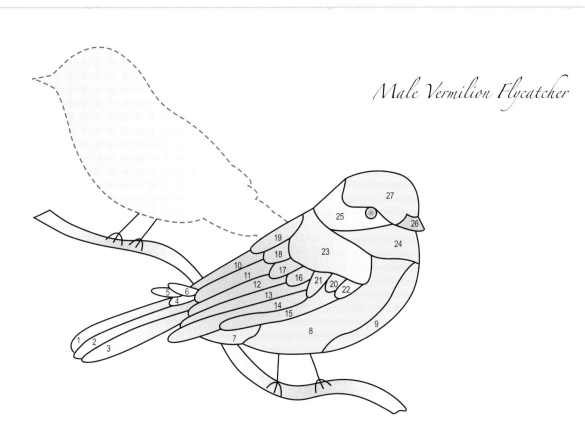

Male Vermilion Flycatcher

Female Vermilion Flycatcher

Painted Bunting

Aptly named, the Painted Bunting is one of the most colorful songbirds. They are found mostly in the south central states and along the Atlantic coastline. Sightings are fairly uncommon as these little birds tend to hide in dense foliage.

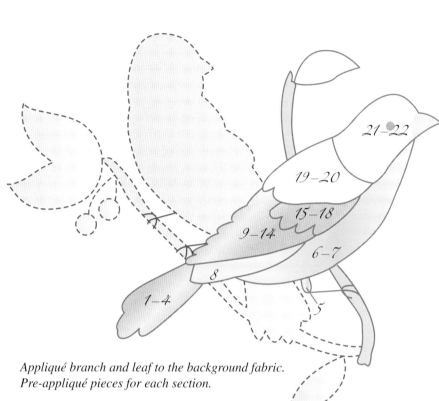

Appliqué branch and leaf to the background fabric.
Pre-appliqué pieces for each section.

Male Painted Bunting

Fabrics
Pieces: 1–3 • 10–12 ◆ Shades of medium brown
Pieces: 4 • 13 ◆ Greenish brown
Pieces: 5–9 ◆ Red
Pieces: 14–15 • 18 ◆ Medium green
Pieces: 16–17 ◆ Light green
Pieces: 19–20 ◆ Yellow, preferably with some
green splotches
Piece: 21 ◆ Gray
Piece: 22 ◆ Blue

Embroidery:
Satin stitch in black for the eye. Outline the eye
in red with stem stitches. Use a double row of
stem stitches in brown for the leg and foot. Stem
stitch in dark gray across the beak.

Female Painted Bunting

Fabrics
Pieces: 1 • 3 • 5 • 9–11 ◆ Shades of medium brown
Pieces: 2 • 4 • 12–15 • 18 ◆ Shades of greenish brown
Piece: 6 ◆ Greenish yellow
Pieces: 7–8 • 16 • 19 ◆ Shades of yellow
Piece: 17 ◆ Gray

Embroidery:
Satin stitch in black for the eye. Use a double row of
stem stitches in brown for the legs and feet and a single
row in green for the berry stems.

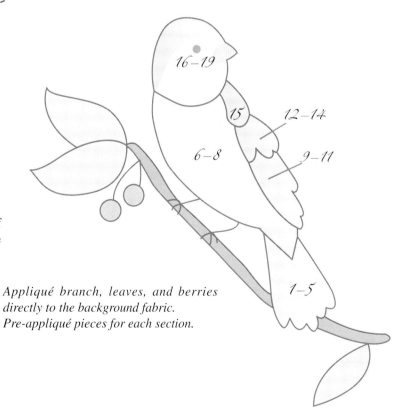

Appliqué branch, leaves, and berries
directly to the background fabric.
Pre-appliqué pieces for each section.

Male Painted Bunting

Female Painted Bunting

This exotic bird is an African Blue Flycatcher found in western Africa. Sometimes called the blue fairy flycatcher, it is distinguished by its crested head and long, fan-like tail. The female also has a crest and fan-like tail but is much grayer than the male.

Male African Blue Flycatcher

Fabrics

Piece: 8 ✧ Pale blue

Pieces: 3 • 6 • 14 • 18 • 21–23 ✧ Light shades of bright blue

Pieces: 2 • 5 • 7 • 17 • 20 • 24 • 26 • 28 ✧ Medium shades of bright blue

Pieces: 1 • 4 • 9 • 13 • 19 • 25 ✧ Dark shades of bright blue

Piece: 27 ✧ Medium gray

Piece: 29 ✧ Black

Pieces: 10–12 • 15–16 ✧ Black with light gray or white highlights

Embroidery:

Satin stitch in black for the eye, then outline the eye with light gray stem stitches. Use a double row of stem stitches in gray for the leg and foot.

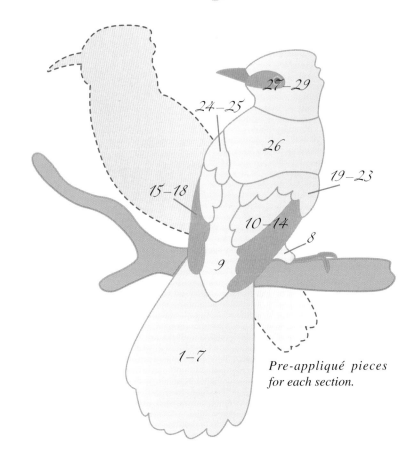

Pre-appliqué pieces for each section.

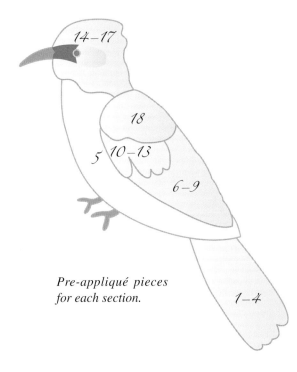

Pre-appliqué pieces for each section.

Female African Blue Flycatcher

Fabrics

Piece: 5 ✧ White with very pale blue splotches

Pieces: 1–4 • 6–13 ✧ Various shades of light blue

Pieces: 14 • 18 ✧ Light blue with a few brown or gray speckles. You can use permanent ink or fabric paint to create the speckles.

Piece: 15 ✧ Dark gray

Piece: 16 ✧ Black

Piece: 17 ✧ Medium blue

Embroidery:

Satin stitch in black for the eye, then outline the eye with light gray stem stitches. Use a double row of stem stitches in gray for the leg and foot.

Male African Blue Flycatcher

Female African Blue Flycatcher

Green Jay

*The Green Jay is mostly found in Mexico and southern Texas. This tropical beauty is about 11"
in length and has a bright yellow belly and outer tail feathers. Males and females look similar.*

Green Jay

Fabrics:

Pieces: 1–2 ◆ Gray
Pieces: 4 • 6 ◆ Light blue
Piece: 5 ◆ Black
Pieces: 14–15 • 17 ◆ Blue
Pieces: 7–8 • 11–12 ◆ Yellow

The remaining pieces are all textured shades of yellowish green ranging from very light to dark. Select some fabrics with white highlights to scatter through the upper wing and tail feathers. If you prefer, white fabric paint can be used to create highlights.

Pieces: 10 • 25 • 33 ◆ Very light yellowish green
Pieces: 3 • 9 • 20 • 22–24 • 31–32 • 43 ◆ Light yellowish green
Pieces: 16 • 18–19 • 28–30 • 34 • 36–37
        ◆ Medium yellowish green
Pieces: 13 • 21 • 26–27 • 35 • 38–42
        ◆ Dark yellowish green

Embroidery:
Use a double or triple row of stem stitches in dark brown for the leg and foot. Satin stitch a small black dot in the eye.

Appliqué branch, leaves, berries, and bird pieces 1 and 2 to the background fabric. Pre-appliqué pieces for each section.

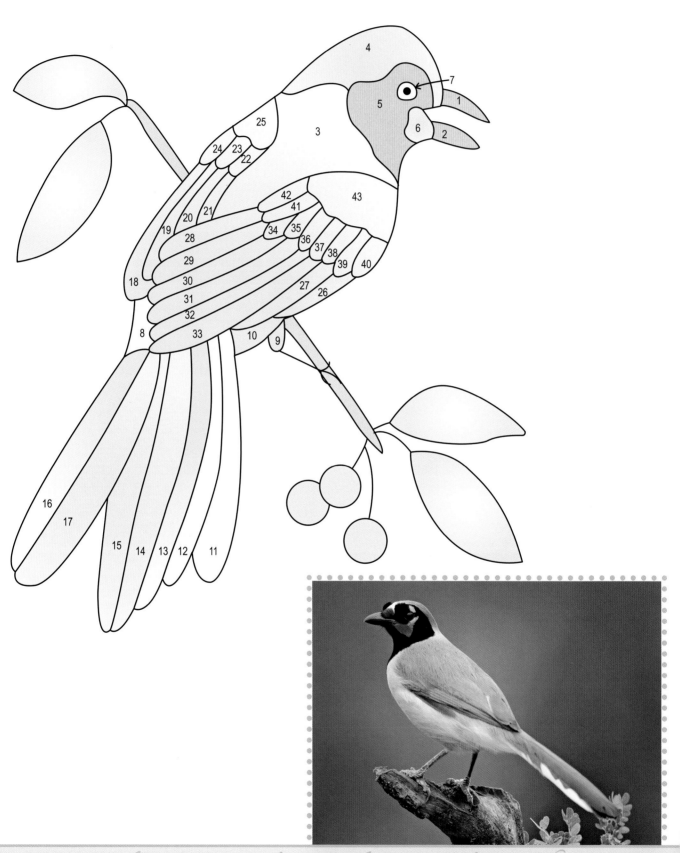

Pine & Evening Grosbeaks

The Pine and Evening Grosbeaks are not closely related, however they are both in the finch family. The Pine Grosbeak is the larger of the two and the Evening Grosbeak is stockier and has a shorter tail. Females of both species are not nearly as colorful as their male counterparts. The females are mostly olive yellow or olive brown with gray underparts.

Pine Grosbeak

Fabrics

Pieces: 1–3 ❖ Medium gray textured with speckles or splotches

Piece: 28 ❖ Light gray textured with speckles or splotches

Pieces: 7 • 21 • 30 ❖ Red

Piece: 31 Dark red

Pieces: 8–12 • 20 ❖ Black-and-white textured. Position fabrics so white is on tips of feathers.

Pieces: 4–6 • 13–19 • 22–27 ❖ Black with white highlights

Piece: 29 ❖ Dark brown

Embroidery:
Satin stitch in black for the eye. Stem stitch in medium brown across the beak. Use a double row of stem stitches in brown for the leg and foot.

Appliqué branch, leaves, and bird piece 1 to the background fabric. Pre-appliqué pieces for each section.

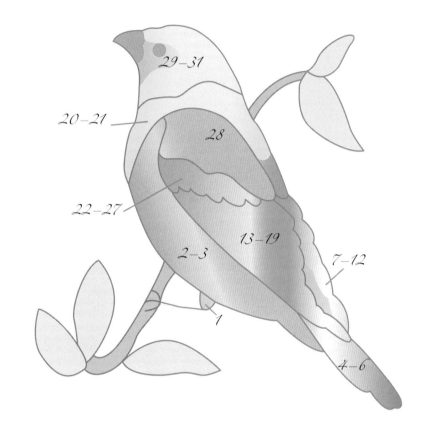

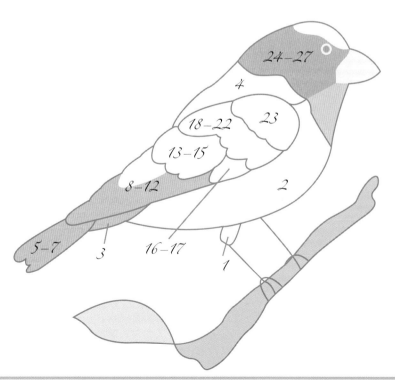

Evening Grosbeak

Fabrics:

Pieces: 1–4 ❖ Shades of medium yellow preferably with gold and/or brown splotches

Pieces: 18–23 • 27 ❖ Yellow textures

Pieces: 11–17 ❖ White

Pieces: 5–10 • 24 • 26 ❖ Black

Piece: 25 ❖ Dark gold

Embroidery:
Satin stitch in black for the eye. Outline the eye in medium gray with stem stitches. Stem stitch in medium brown across the beak. Use a double row of stem stitches in brown for the legs and feet.

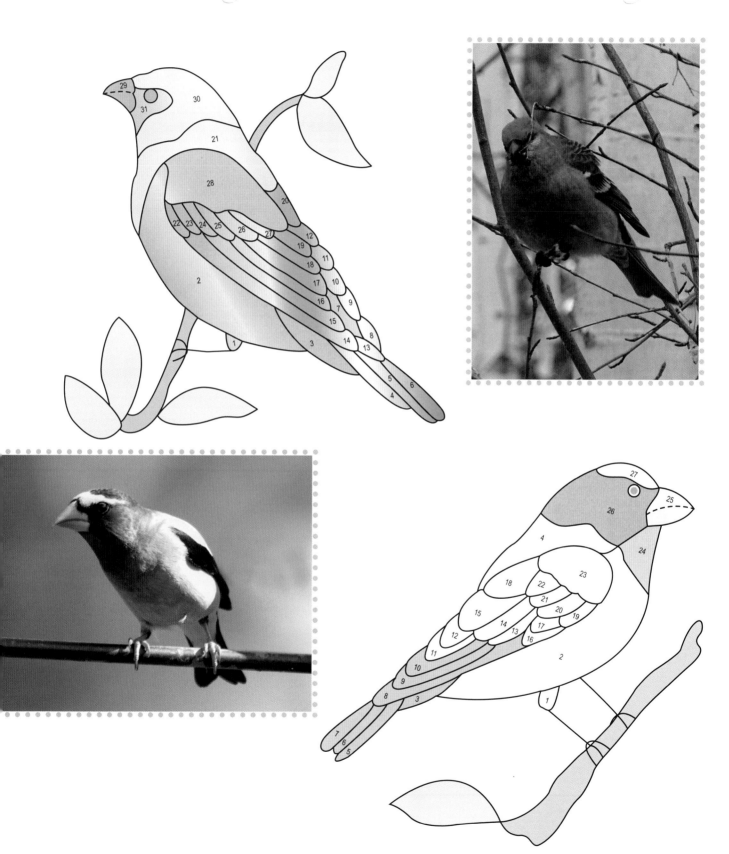

Start with center unit.

*Reverse the appliqué pattern
for left side of border.*

*Reverse the appliqué pattern
for left side of border.*

*Reverse the appliqué pattern
for left side of border.*

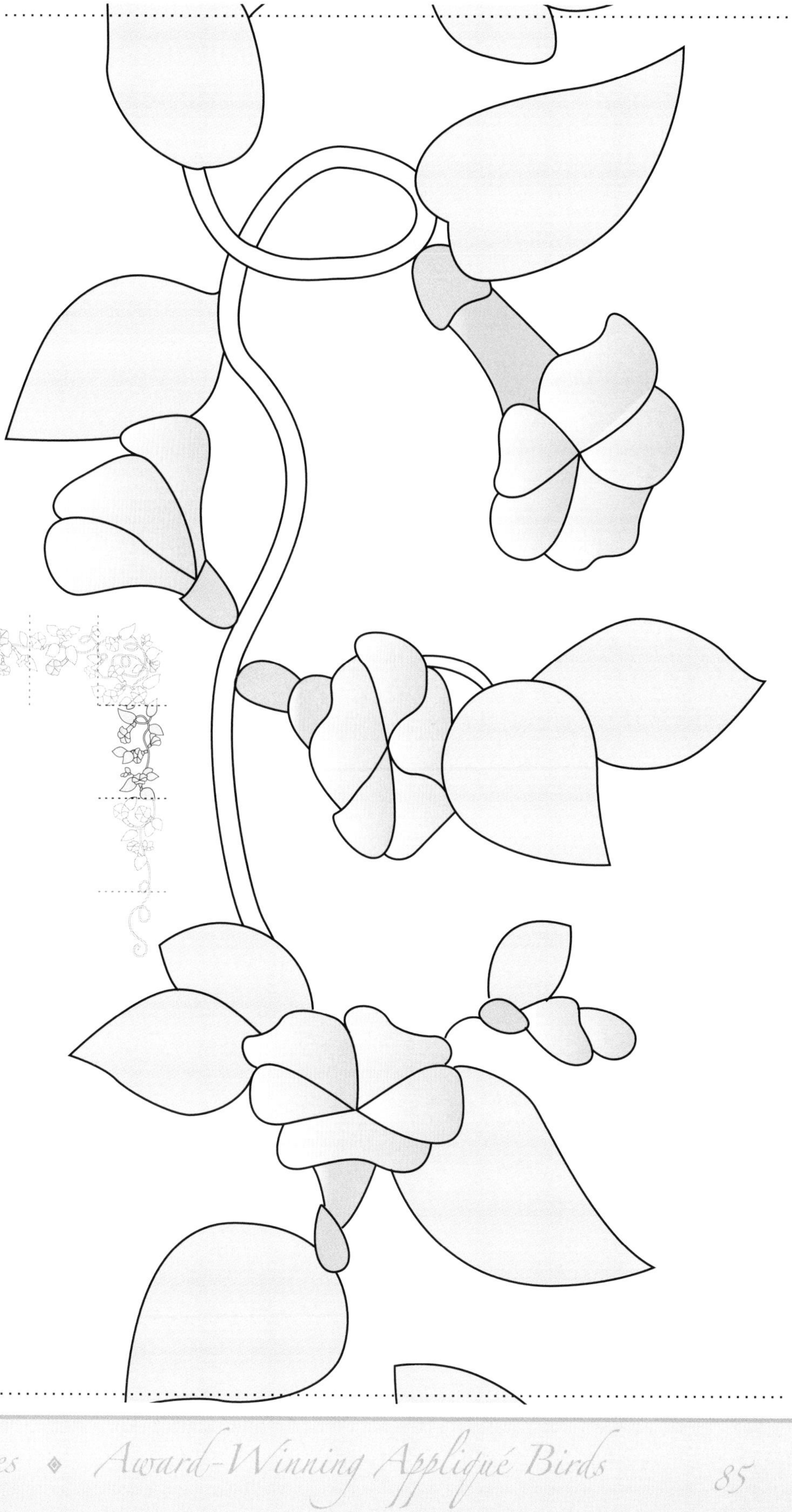

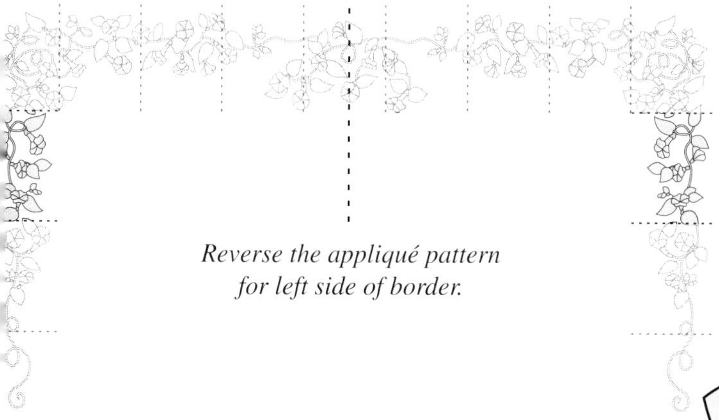

Reverse the appliqué pattern for left side of border.

Reverse the appliqué pattern
for left side of border.

Reverse the appliqué pattern
for left side of border.

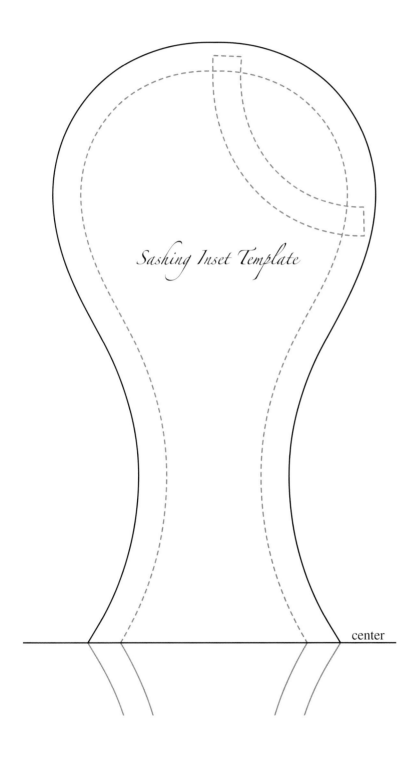

Sashing Inset Template

center

Sashing Inset Template

Trace and cut along the outside line for the sashing insets.

The dotted line indicates the bias tape placement.

Add an extra segment of bias tape, as indicated on the template, along the outside edges of the nine-block unit, to finish the four loop clusters.

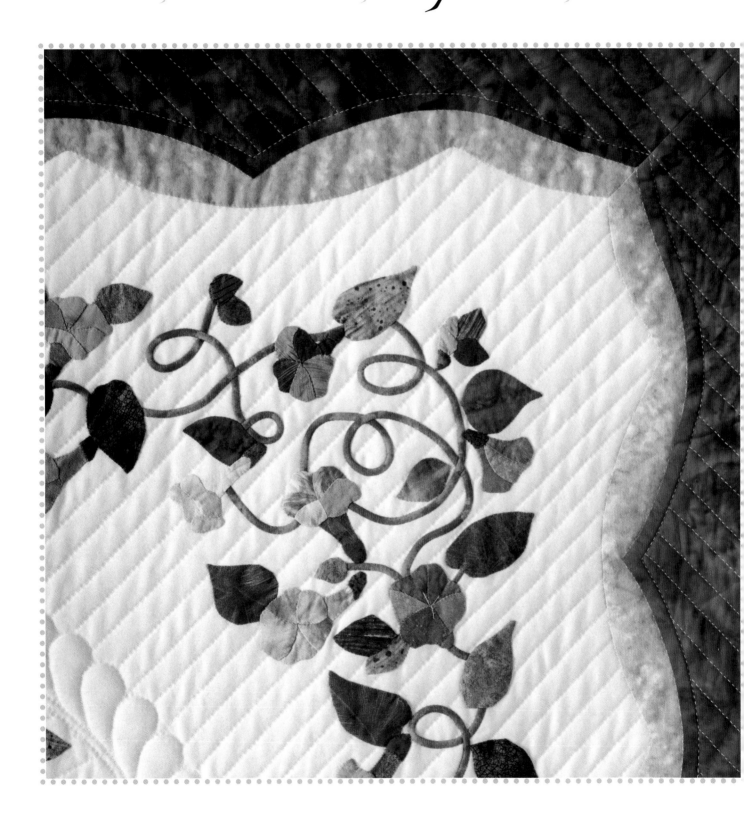

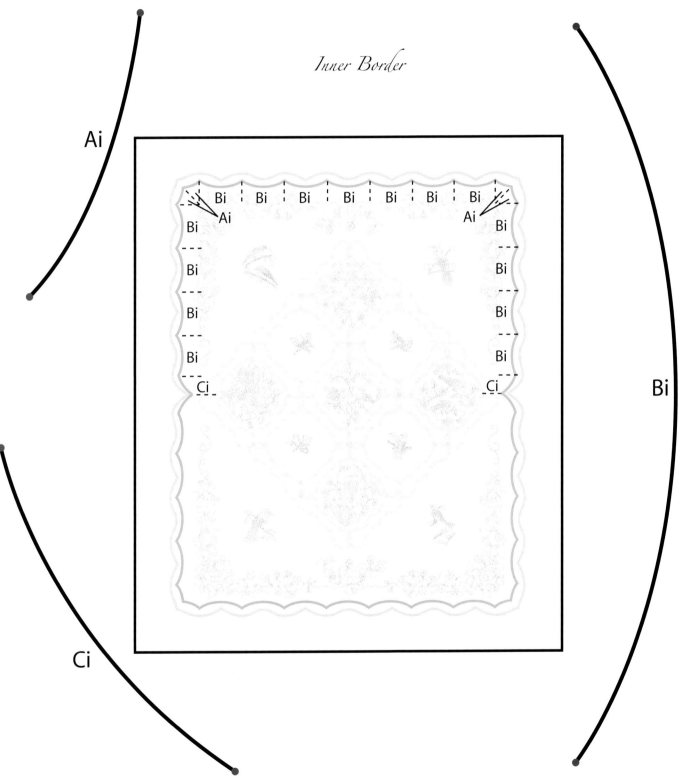

Inner Border

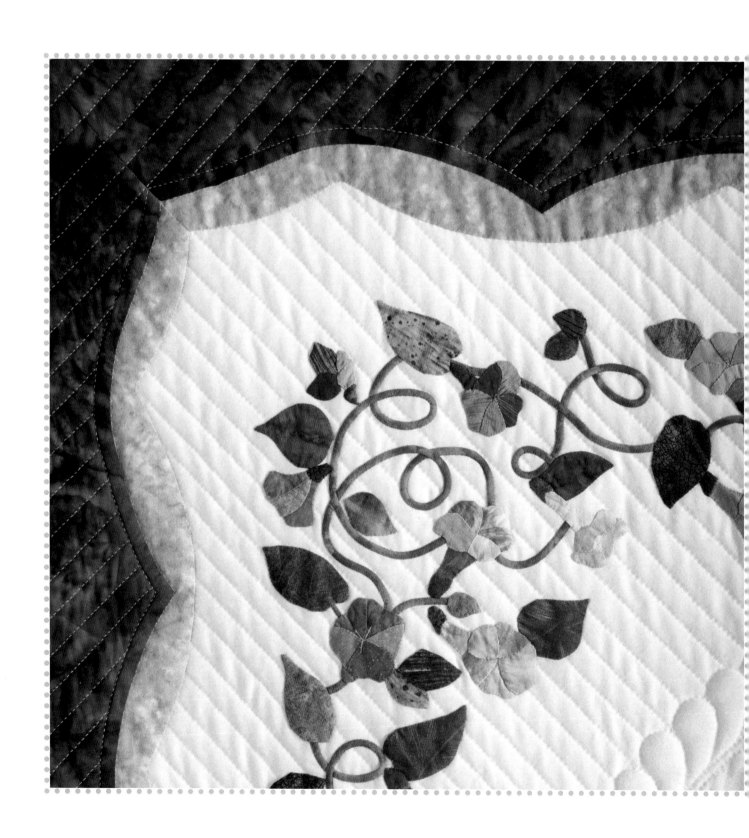

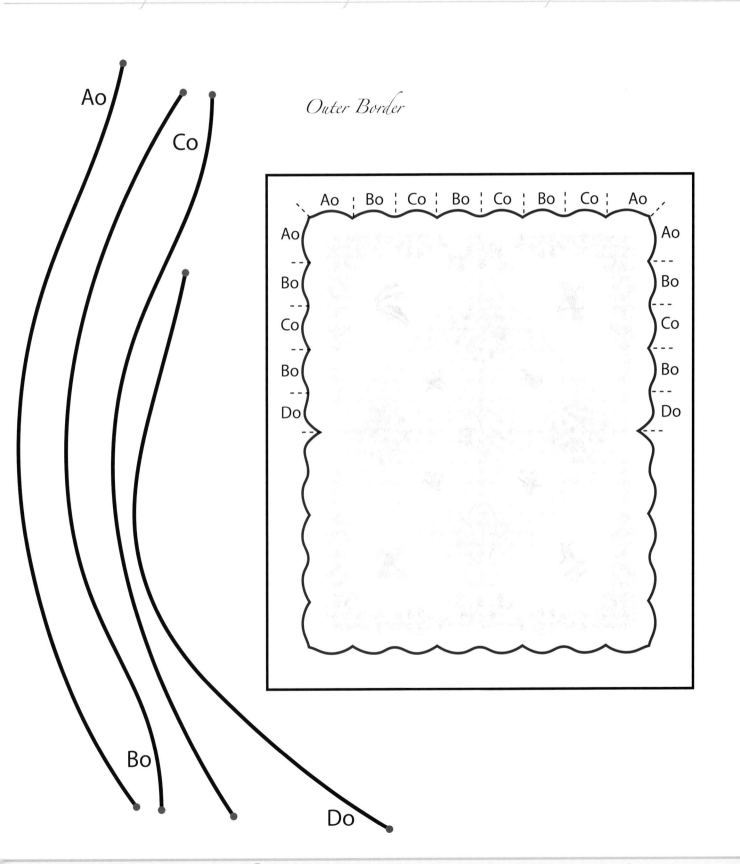

Ao

Co

Bo

Do

Outer Border

Ao | Bo | Co | Bo | Co | Bo | Co | Ao

Ao
Bo
Co
Bo
Do

Ao
Bo
Co
Bo
Do

Pamela Humphries

Newly retired after 32 years as a communications consultant, Pamela, a non-sewer other than buttons and hems, happened to watch an episode of *Simply Quilts* in 1999 and a new passion was born. She started with machine piecing but found it too frustrating and never finished that first quilt. A decision to try it by hand was the solution, and amazingly, this masterpiece is only Pamela's second handmade quilt.

Pamela loves bird-watching and other outdoor activities, and she studied field guides and photographs before making original drawings for the 24 birds. Using mostly large-scale printed commercial fabrics to achieve subtle shading effects, Pamela constructed each bird using needle-turn appliqué and then sewed the finished units to the background.

Pamela's favorite part of the process is hand quilting, and she spent over one thousand hours quilting this piece. When working on FEATHERED BEAUTIES, she quilted for eight hours a day, taking occasional breaks for lunch, exercise, and playing with her dog. Pamela is thrilled that her quilt is a part of the permanent collection of the Museum of the American Quilter's Society.

Other AQS Books

This is only a small selection of the books available from the American Quilter's Society. AQS books are known worldwide for timely topics, clear writing, beautiful color photos, and accurate illustrations and patterns. The following books are available from your local bookseller, quilt shop, or public library.

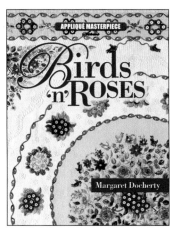

#7013   us$24.95

#6211   us$19.95

#5338   us$21.95

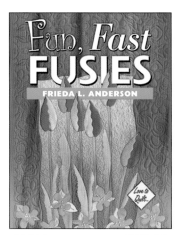

#6801   us$19.95

#6904   us$21.95

#6674   us$19.95

#7073   us$24.95

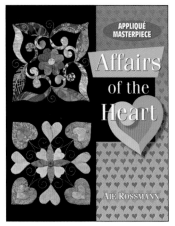

#6517   us$21.95

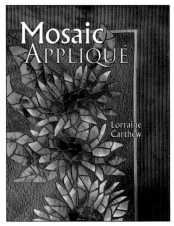

#7071   us$22.95